Get set... GO!

Autumn

Ruth Thomson

Contents

W

FRANKLIN WATTS

LONDON • NEW YORK • SYDNEY

It's autumn!

Autumn is a time of change.
The days become shorter and colder.
The leaves of trees and bushes turn
orange, yellow and brown and fall off.

The hedgerows are bright
with rosehips and berries.
The ground is littered with acorns
and conkers and other seeds.

Many birds fly away
to warmer countries for the winter.
Squirrels, mice and voles gather
stores of food and bury them.

Bats, frogs, snakes and dormice
find a sheltered place.
They go into a deep sleep,
called hibernation.

A leaf collection

Get ready

✔ Leaves   ✔ Heavy books   ✔ Scrapbook

✔ Newspaper   ✔ Glue   ✔ Felt-tip pen

...Get set

Collect all sorts of fallen leaves.
Look carefully to find out
which trees they have come from.

⇒ ⇒ ⇒ *Go!*

Lay the leaves between
two sheets of newspaper.
Put heavy books on top.
After two weeks, the leaves
will be flat and dry.
Glue them in a scrapbook and label them.

Cappadocian Maple

Hawthorn

Red Oak

Alder

Willow

Sweet Chestnut

Mountain Ash (Rowan)

Cherry

Autumn tree collage

Get ready

✔ Strong, thin paper

✔ Masking tape

✔ Wax crayons

✔ Leaves

✔ Scissors

✔ Glue

✔ Blue paper

...Get set

Tape thin paper to a tree trunk.
Rub a wax crayon over it.
A pattern will appear.
Dry some leaves (see page 4).

Go!

Cut out a trunk from your bark rubbing.
Glue it on to the blue paper.
Glue on the dried leaves.

A leafy face

Get ready

✔ Sheet of stiff,   ✔ Leaves
   coloured paper   ✔ Glue

...Get set

Dry some leaves (see page 4).
Sort them by colour, size and shape.

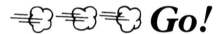 **Go!**

Arrange the leaves on the paper
in the shape of a face.
When you are happy with it,
glue the leaves in position.

Salt dough models

Get ready

✔ 2 cups plain flour   ✔ 1 cup cold water   ✔ Food colourings

✔ 1 cup salt   ✔ 2 tablespoons cooking oil   ✔ Baking tray

...Get set

Stir the ingredients in a bowl.
Knead the mixture with your hands.
Make several small balls of dough.
Add drops of food colouring.
Knead until the colour is mixed in.

⇒💨⇒💨⇒💨 *Go!*

Shape the dough and cut and prick it
with a knife or fork to make patterns.
Bake it in the oven on a baking tray
at 300°F/150°C for at least an hour.

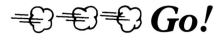

10

 # A fruit and seed collectio

Get ready

✔ All sorts of fruits and seeds
   from trees, bushes and flowers

...Get set

Open some of the fruit to see
the seeds inside.
Keep pine cones in a warm, dry place.
Soon they will open, so you can see
their seeds.

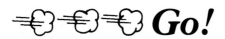 ***Go!***

Find out the names of
your fruits and seeds.
Label your collection.

Sweet
Chestnuts

Horse Chestnuts

Beech fruits

Plane seeds

Sycamore
wings

Ash
keys

Broom pods

Scots Pine
cones

Birch
seeds

Oak
acorns

Ivy seeds

Rosehips

See how seeds scatter

Get ready

✔ All sorts of fruit and seeds

...Get set

Sort your collection into groups.

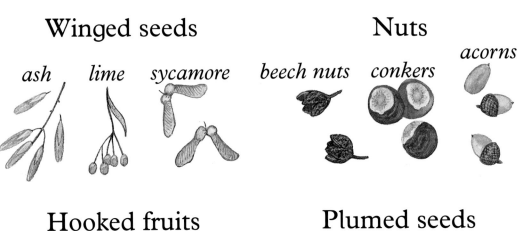

Winged seeds

ash   *lime*   *sycamore*

Nuts

beech nuts   *conkers*   *acorns*

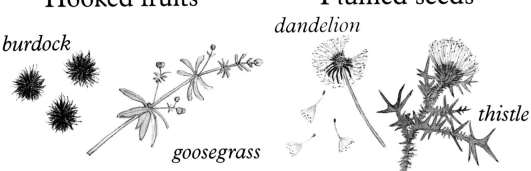

Hooked fruits

burdock

goosegrass

Plumed seeds

dandelion

thistle

Go!

Throw winged seeds up in the air. Measure how far they travel.

See how nuts are protected. Count the seeds in each case.

See what hooked fruits cling to. Try wood, fur, wool, plastic and metal.

Blow a plumed seed head. Watch where the seeds go.

# Seed picture

Get ready

✔ Flat seeds: ash, sycamore, elm, pumpkin, sunflower

✔ Sheet of stiff paper
✔ Pencil
✔ Glue

...Get set

Draw the outline of a picture
faintly, in pencil.
Spread glue inside it.
Sort your seeds by size and shape.

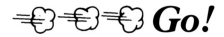 **Go!**

Stick seeds on to your picture.
Start at the edges and cover the outline.

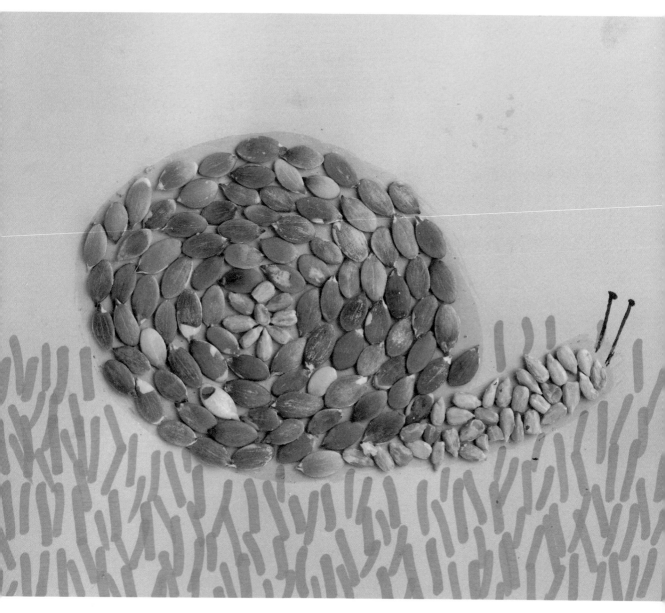

Autumn picture

Get ready

✔ 1 m of 1"(2.5 cm) wide wood

✔ Nails

✔ Hammer

✔ Wood glue

✔ Wood stain or paint

✔ Stapler

✔ Leaves, twigs, seeds, berries

✔ String

...Get set

Ask an adult to cut the wood
into four equal pieces.
Nail and glue it to make a frame.
Paint or stain it.

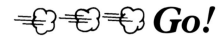 **Go!**

Staple leaves, twigs and seeds
on to the back of the frame.
Hang berries on some string.

Vegetable kebabs

Get ready

✔ Peppers   ✔ Baby sweetcorn   ✔ Knife

✔ Courgettes   ✔ Olive oil   ✔ Tablespoon

✔ Mushrooms   ✔ Lemon   ✔ Dish

✔ Cherry tomatoes   ✔ Lemon squeezer   ✔ Skewers

...Get set

Chop the courgettes and peppers.
Pour 3 spoons of oil into the dish.
Cut the lemon in half and squeeze it.
Mix 3 spoons of the juice with the oil.
Soak the vegetables in this mixture for 2 hours.

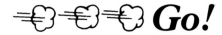 ## Go!

Thread the vegetables on to skewers.
Grill them for 8 minutes, turning often.

Woodland masks

Get ready

✔ Newspaper torn into strips

✔ Large balloon

✔ Wallpaper paste

✔ Scissors

✔ Paints and paintbrush

✔ Thin elastic

✔ Leaves, seeds and feathers to decorate

...Get set

Paste several layers of newspaper strips over half a blown-up balloon. Leave them to dry for several days.

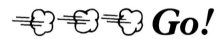 Go!

Take out the balloon.
Cut eye, nose and mouth holes in the mask.
Paint and decorate it.
Make a hole on either side.
Thread the elastic through and knot it.